To El...
My Angel, Fri...
Mentor

Thank you,
Joyce A. Smith

In Search of Higher Grounds

JoyAnn

authorHOUSE®

AuthorHouse™
1663 Liberty Drive, Suite 200
Bloomington, IN 47403
www.authorhouse.com
Phone: 1-800-839-8640

© 2009 JoyAnn. All rights reserved.

No part of this book may be reproduced, stored in a retrieval system, or transmitted by any means without the written permission of the author.

First published by AuthorHouse 4/30/2009

ISBN: 978-1-4389-2495-3 (sc)

Printed in the United States of America
Bloomington, Indiana

This book is printed on acid-free paper.

This frustrating, detailed, yet sometimes humorous narrative is dedicated to the millions who successfully survived the perils of Hurricane Katrina and to those who are still struggling. Never, never, never give up, for nothing is mightier than God's Holy Hand.

The events depicted herein are true, as best recalled by the author. However, some incidents have been altered for clarity, omitted for brevity, and changed for security.

Special thanks to J. Arnold, for helping keep past and present tense in relevant order.

ABOUT THE AUTHOR

JoyAnn is a resident of New Orleans, Louisiana; she has temporarily relocated to Bryant, Arkansas via the aftermath of Hurricane Katrina. After dropping out of high school and working numerous minimum wage jobs, Joy returned to school; She enrolled in night classes and received a General Education Diploma. Later, she joined the Army Reserves to help finance and continue her education. She received a Business Diploma from a local Tech School, went to Delgado Community College and next transferred to the University of New Orleans. She continued working while attending college at night. After earning over 400 hours of credit, she was advised to switch to day classes in order to receive a degree. Night classes, it turned out, was strictly a convenience; it did not offer full curricula which would net a degree. This was upsetting, however, life went on- -jobs and lifestyle improved. After twenty years of military service, Joy retired from the Louisiana Army National Guard at the rank of Sergeant First Class. Currently, she has more than twenty-six years of federal service and is looking forward to retirement from the US Postal Service. Although a novice writer, she spends many hours inaundating and entertaining friends and family with letters, poems, and short stories. Over the years, JoyAnn has entered numerous literary and playwriting contests. She has not won, but received some recognition. One of her entries was read at the Contemporary Arts Center, New Orleans; she also received a notation from Terry Meagan, a playwriting judge. Ms. Meagan commendeded Joy's strong writing abilities and meticulous sense for details. While living in New Orleans, Joy participated in countless drama activities hosted by her church, Beecher Memorial, UCC. Moreover, one of JoyAnn's favorite pastimes is to share comments and swap critiques pertaining to popular movies and plays.

CHAPTER 1

You, no doubt, will agree that Hurricane Katrina was one of the most devastating events to occur in our country's history. In the beginning, the focus was on the despair and anguish suffered by Katrina's victims. Immediately thereafter, many Americans watched, in horror, media coverage that depicted the ignorance and disorganization of government officials as they slowly began to offer relief to hurricane survivors. However, once this initial shock wore off, the finger pointing began.

Mental duress, physical exhaustion, loss of lives, and destruction of property are a few examples of what victims suffered. I am Jane Nelson, a New Orleans native. I have lived there all my life; suffice it to say, I am well past fifty years old. I consider myself modern-minded and physically capable—with the exception of a recent hip replacement. Up until Katrina, I also judged my character to be independent, selectively stubborn, and occasionally risqué. Moreover, I am a homeowner, strategically courteous, and a law-abiding citizen. I am also Afro-American, single, retired military, and employed by the U.S. Postal Service.

Moreover, although I strive to maintain an independent yet realistic lifestyle, my struggle with Christianity has always been problematic. Perhaps it was my childhood, but more than likely, it was my heritage. My family has always been dysfunctional, even before the term became popular. As a small child, I was shy and sometimes mistrusting of others. I was confused and often frightened by signs of open affection. Nonetheless, from an early age, I was able to deduce that our family was somewhat unorthodox. Our biological mother was never an intricate part of our lives. My dad, an immigrant, was not very affectionate. His English was barely comprehensible, his temper was fierce, and his practice of Christianity did not exist. However, in order to fit into the American lifestyle that he'd chosen, he felt it necessary to ensure that his offspring attended school and church regularly. The school thing I understood, but the necessity of church eluded me.

Further, the lesson being taught in church did not carry over into my life. For in my world, I felt abandoned—alone. "If God exists," I challenged, "what are the criteria for His love?" Still, there could be no denying that there was a greater power at hand, for there were numerous unexplained occurrences. Nonetheless, I maintained, "If there is a God, why is there so much unhappiness?" I concluded that God was intangible idealism.

As I grew older, I learned to accept good and bad, without explanation, as they occurred. I told myself that I was mature and therefore responsible for my own fate. I could discern between good and evil, and I tried to conduct myself accordingly. I gave up attending church, because I just didn't get it. But eventually this crisis-filled world got *me*. As such, I came full circle to where my journey had begun: running toward the unknown. My life was heavily burdened, there were numerous unanswered developments, and I was filled with emotional despair. Although I was nowhere near atonement, I stretched out my hands in desperation. I invited Jesus into my world because I was overwhelmed by the stress of everyday living. I needed purpose and direction. Although my reason for accepting Christ may not have been idealistic, He heard my plea and gave me the peace I desired. Nonetheless, I continued to struggle with theology, but having Jesus at the helm made it a more comfortable voyage.

But things were about to get rough. I had no idea that my mustard-seed leap of faith was about to be tested. Although I had invited Him into my life, my spirit remained inactive. I considered my tithes, church attendance, and prayers to be proof of reclaimed Christianity, yet my life had no significant variation; I was still calculative and unconcerned. However, Katrina put a different spin on my world. Surviving the perils of Katrina and its wake not only reemphasized God's powers, but it also armored me with patience, humbleness, and quiet acceptance. Moreover, when evacuated from my roof, taken to the Convention Center in New Orleans, and later flown to Arkansas, I also experienced the joy of being blessed!

CHAPTER 2

It has been a little over two years since Katrina blew into my life, and since that time, I've been introduced to other attributes of living. I am currently residing in Bryant, Arkansas, a small, rustic community with an estimated population of twelve thousand! I have seen some blacks, but, by far, the majority of the population is white. Quite naturally, upon my arrival I wasn't engrossed nor affected by demographics. Instead, I was consumed with grief and need. Above all, I was just thankful to be alive, and I could do nothing more than praise God for His infinite goodness and wisdom.

But I digress. One should never begin a story from the middle. It's just that I have lived this story nearly every waking moment since Katrina's onset, and sometimes I prefer to dally over the highlights rather than keep the information flowing in a natural order. Katrina hit the Gulf Coast—in particular, New Orleans—on Monday morning, August 29, 2005, at approximately one in the morning. I was at home—alone. Why?

I, unfortunately, did not believe the hype. As previously stated, I have lived in New Orleans all my life, perhaps I'd become arrogant and complacent, but most assuredly I was ignorant.

CHAPTER 3

Admittedly, there had been much media coverage spotlighting Hurricane Katrina and detailing possible outcomes. But everything being reported had been said thousands of times before. Quite frankly, all storms, from depressions to elevated categories, that somehow found their way into the Gulf, have always been touted as Armageddon. Moreover, some broadcasters seemed to delight in crying wolf during these events as a means of hogging air time. That is to say, if the local news had been sluggish, then placing undue emphasis on approaching storms would certainly be a way of monopolizing public attention. And some of their methods of reporting had been, on such occasions, much like those of snake oil salesmen. Over the years, I had pretty much heard and seen it all. So when the newscasters, politicians, and emergency officials began hawking a full city evacuation, I chalked it up as routine shenanigans. Furthermore, I had never before evacuated during a storm. And I believe the worse storms thus far in my lifetime prior to Katrina had been Betsy and Camille. Of course, I am no expert on these historic events. I was young, a student, when these hurricanes swept across the Gulf Coast. Nonetheless, I can recall Betsy; I remember the crying, tales of woe, and rescue efforts. But what is most memorable is the fact that due to Betsy, the school I attended closed for three additional months. I was ecstatic. You see, we were just ending summer vacation and were preparing to enter the fall semester. My high school was located in the Lower Ninth Ward and had incurred substantial water damage; therefore, we were given additional time out of school while renovations ensued. Further, over the years, hurricanes, although unpredictable forces, had never made that much of an impact on me. I am not saying I didn't respect them, but I never felt the need to flee them either. In other words, I was content to live in uninformed bliss.

CHAPTER 4

As I matured and dealt with adult responsibilities, hurricanes more or less became nuisances. I had learned to live with the inconvenience and discomfort associated with these storms: namely the aftermath. Their disruptions usually consisted of power outages, called brownouts; a backlog of sanitation pick-ups; irregular or nonexistent public transportation; and the awkwardness of school and business closings. Unlike my childhood, I no longer embraced hurricanes; instead, I began to view them as annoyances.

Accordingly, when did I wise up, you may be asking? I believe it was around eleven o'clock that Sunday night, August 28, 2005. My relatives, at least the few who still resided in New Orleans, and most of my friends, had already left town. Before their departure, some had approached me with offers of traveling with them, but I scoffed and waved them off. Besides, I had plans: a three-day excursion to Biloxi, Mississippi! On that Sunday, I was flipping through broadcasts to determine whether or not my scheduled trip would still be possible.

Unfortunately, the reports were not encouraging. The storm, it seemed, was headed directly toward the Gulf Coast. Moreover, newscasters were reporting that Interstate Highway Ten (I-10) heading east had been closed due to bad weather. Authorities were requesting that travelers find alternate routes. Thus, my trip was ruined.

Biloxi, you see, was directly in the storm's path. I was not familiar with any route leading out of town other than I-10 East. As such, I decided to ride out the storm at home and reschedule the trip for a later date. The reports continued. Broadcasters asked citizens who still remained in their homes to make their way to the Superdome. They announced that city officials had opened the Dome as a last-minute shelter. In addition, an anchorman announced that stations were ending their broadcasts. Moreover, they warned that viewers who declined to seek shelter at the Dome would be responsible for their own safety. But they also said that rescue helicopters would be flying in and around the metropolitan area immediately after the storm. If rescue was desired, then viewers should access their roofs and attempt to signal aerial support. It was further stated that due to the severe weather, city newsrooms were evacuating their employees and Baton Rouge stations would continue airing storm coverage.

CHAPTER 5

This was a twist! After all these years of living in New Orleans, not once had I heard of any news station ending its broadcasts in the middle of a storm—and evacuating its employees. What type of nonsense was this? Immediately I turned to other channels. They, too, were ending broadcasts. Reality began to creep in. This storm must be serious; otherwise these reporters would never leave the anchor desk. In fact, if anything, they seem to relish competing for airtime. But now they were announcing abandonment? Fleeing the city? What was going on?

Perhaps I needed to rethink evacuation. A million thoughts flooded my brain. Where should I go? Certainly not the Dome! I knew that inner-city traffic was going to be horrendous. And once at the Dome, where could I park my car? My vision of being trapped in the Superdome with thousands of hysterical citizens was undesirable. I thought about chancing out-of-town traffic. But how much time did I have? Where would I go? Didn't an earlier report inform me that I-10 East had been closed? What about westbound traffic? Wasn't there something about detours and blockage? I wasn't scared—yet! But it was beginning to sink in: perhaps I'd made a mistake. The newsrooms were closing. The news crews were leaving, and most of the familiar roads were not accessible. What should I do?

Well, first of all, I reasoned to myself, *Calm down! So what if the local stations are closing or if this storm is bigger than anticipated? I will be okay. I have water, electricity, and food. Just remain calm. Morning will be here shortly.* With that logic intact, I halted my momentary insanity and returned my attention to the broadcasts. It was then that my ears detected the moaning of the wind and the heavy downpour of rain. Nonetheless, I remained unnerved. The noise from the rain and the clamor of the wind increased. Suddenly, there was a loud explosion. My lights went out, and the television blackened! Evidently, an electric transformer had blown. Now I was in the dark, and to make matters worse, the winds picked up—whipping, twirling, and crashing. The noise was deafening. There was no pretending: my fear was undeniable. A huge tree limb fell onto my roof, cracking and leaving a small hole into which rainwater seeped. Wooden shutters were ripped from my windows and tossed about like cardboard. Outdoors, garbage cans and other unsecured properties were thrown about dizzily. The sounds of the wind increased. At times, it sounded like the amplified howls of ghosts or other such night creatures depicted in horror movies. Moreover, it had the eerie pitch of a derailed locomotive.

 I began to pray. With the television off, no lights, and the ghastly sounds, I was besieged with fright. I don't know how long it lasted; I can remember only being relieved when an unnatural quiet ensued. The winds ceased. I ventured to the front door to peer out. It was as I suspected. Tree limbs, garbage cans, and miscellaneous debris cluttered the sidewalk and streets. I am not Catholic, yet I made the sign of the cross. I smiled. Though it was still raining, I hoped that the storm had ended. And although I still had no lights, I was nonetheless relieved. *Okay,* I told myself, *this isn't so bad.*

CHAPTER 6

It was at this point that the incessant rain became a deluge. *Even so,* I reasoned, *what's a little water?* Not quite an hour later, my question was answered. The rain persisted and became torrential. My damaged roof now leaked profusely. I was no longer confident, but I still managed a small snicker. After all, I'd had my home insurance for over twenty years and had never filed a claim. So if damaged shutters, roof, walls, and carpet were the only things affected, then it was a small sacrifice.

Hours later, the rain persisted. I began to tire of its presence, but I continued to monitor the level of water outside my home. I became increasingly anxious as the water rose above street level and began to flow toward front lawns. *Okay, so when is this going to end?* I pondered. As a New Orleans native, I had experienced flood conditions before, but never beyond street and sidewalk levels. This flooding had already surpassed that. Thus, I began to pace. I'd accepted the damaged roof and carpet, but if the rain did not stop, what else would be sacrificed? At about four o'clock that morning, the rain became less intense, and by six o'clock it ended.

I sent up praises! *Ha! I made it! Those television idiots were only trying to scare me.* Though admittedly this had been the worst I'd experienced. I had survived unscathed, albeit shaken. I ventured outdoors; the water level was still unnaturally high. I surveyed the damage. *I can live with this,* I concluded. Granted, the streets were flooded, and I had no electricity, gas, or working phone, but I did have food and running water. So what to do? I decided to take a bath and then a nap. After all that praying and worrying, I was exhausted. The bath was cold, but I was hoping it would relax me. Just before laying down, I went outside to check the water level. Strangely, it seemed elevated. I thought it was my imagination. There was no rain or wind. The hurricane was over—wasn't it? So how could the water be higher? I reasoned that I just needed to rest. But I couldn't sleep. The water level kept ebbing into my thoughts. From time to time, I'd get up to check. Inevitably, the water was indeed rising.

CHAPTER 7

By noon the water was no longer at the edges of lawns; it had begun to encroach upon the foundations of homes. As I paced back and forth, my mind entertained and probed every aspect of fear. I was momentarily halted, however, by what sounded like a thud. The noise was reverberating yet muffled. I peered outside, trying to get a fix on its origin, but nothing seemed out of kilter. I had to get a grip on my nerves. The sound was frightening, yet there was nothing physical to which I could attribute the need for urgency. I turned slightly away from the door, my attention drawn back to the anxieties already at hand. But before I could complete my pivot, I caught a glimpse of what appeared to be frantic splashing. I was somewhat surprised and fearful. Thus far, I had not considered that someone else could be stuck in their home, on my block, and sharing my predicament. Now, just after this horrific thud, I saw for the first time another sign of life. This splashing was huge!

I ventured out of my home and onto the paved walkway that connected to my drive. The cement walkway was paved on an incline, and the highest section was closest to my door; therefore, although the water had been rising, it had not yet encompassed this point. I stood at the apex of the walkway and peered toward the heavy splattering. It must have been about one o'clock PM. The atmosphere was shadowy.

I eventually made out the form responsible for the watery interruption. It was a man. He ran full-throttle toward me, but on the opposite side of the street. The legs of his pants were rolled bulkily. A pair of brown shoes was tucked awkwardly under one arm, while his other arm swung and pumped the air uncontrollably. His face was frantic; his expression gothic. *Now what?* I asked myself. This guy scared me. I couldn't tell if he was running from or toward something. I began to wonder if I should be running, too. I was not certain if he saw me or not. Nonetheless, I returned to the safety of my home.

As for the noise, I was clueless, but seeing the liquid sprinter definitely honed my need for security. As I crossed the threshold, I noticed that the water had made its way inside my home. The floor was a shallow pool. This was a nightmare, and I couldn't wake up! The water was ankle deep. *I've got to get out of here*, I agonized. The water began making wakes and waves around me. Things were falling—slipping. Moreover, the water continued to elevate at an alarming rate, lapping my thighs and threatening my instinct for survival. *Get to the roof! Isn't that what the newscasters advised?* It took a whole lot of conviction and every bit of my strength to eventually get onto the roof, but I did what was necessary to survive. I managed to put aside my growing fears and vanquish my natural instinct to nurse my ailing hip. Instead, I gathered my overnight bag, a flashlight, my walking cane, and a ten-foot aluminum ladder. I leaned the ladder against the rear of my home and very timidly pulled myself upward, rung by rung, until I found myself atop and at the roof's edge.

Once there, new fears plagued me. I hadn't anticipated the incline of the roof, which prevented me from standing or walking. I was stuck at the edge! I had my cane, but my inability to move was increased by my fear of heights and the medical restraints of having had a hip replacement. Thus, I sat there, seemingly for hours, surveying my predicament. It was approximately 8:00 PM; the stars and moon lit up the sky, yet I was surrounded by darkness, wetness, and silence. *Okay, so I am on the roof. What now? I* pondered. I looked at the water, which now seemed to have devoured everything in sight. *How high will it get?* I wondered. *If I had to, could I crawl any higher?* I agonized. But my mental conference was halted abruptly as my ears picked up the annoying buzzing of hungry mosquitoes. They swarmed madly, surrounding me, diving and biting relentlessly. "I can not believe this!" I nearly screamed. Here I was precariously perched atop my roof, barely holding on to sanity, yet alone safety, and amid this crucial turmoil were mosquitoes! I began slapping at my face and arms. My legs, too, were under attack. But unfortunately, my physical condition did not allow full protection of these areas. The best I could do was to shake my dangled legs in an erratic pattern. I was hoping that perpetual movement would ward off the tenacious attackers. "What now, Lord?" I asked.

CHAPTER 8

As though in response to my question, I heard what at first sounded like the distant roar of a small engine. As the sounds became more distinct and louder, I cast my eyes upward and discovered the source. Along with the stars and moon, the sky now showcased helicopters. They were everywhere, flying to and fro and circling. Immediately I forgot about the mosquitoes! I reached for my flashlight and began signaling. *Saved!* I thought while offering up a silent prayer. I flashed over and over again; however, the helicopters did not return my signals. Nonetheless, I continued to flash until the stars and moon were once again the only luminaries in the sky. *"Did they see me?"* I wondered. *"Will they come back?"* I worried. But I had no chance to respond to self query, because the mosquitoes once again had my attention.

They vengefully attacked every exposed surface of my body. I slapped, shook, and scratched incessantly. But then my attention wavered again, for in the distance, I saw a light. It was moving perpendicular to my position but nonetheless moving. I knew it couldn't be a car; the streets were too flooded. I reasoned that it couldn't be a helicopter; there was not enough space to support a landing. My curiosity and need for survival overtook me. "Hello!" I cried out. But no one answered. "Hello!" I offered again.

This time there was a response: "Hello!"

Bless my soul! I nearly tumbled off the roof. "Help me!" I anxiously pleaded.

"Where are you?" A male voice questioned.

"I am on the roof," I replied.

"Do you have a flashlight?" The masculine voice asked.

"Yes," I responded, and I then quickly clicked it on.

"I see you," the voice assured. "I am in a boat," he advised. "I am coming to get you," he promised. I was elated. I was going to be saved. Next, the man in the boat explained that he would have to come back, because he had too many people already on board. He promised to return; so I sat there for what seemed like forever, waiting to be rescued.

During the time before my Samaritan returned, I staved off the bloodthirsty mosquitoes and managed to keep my sanity as I watched numerous rescue helicopters fly obliviously above me.

CHAPTER 9

Just before the resurgence of my insecurities, the light reappeared. The boater had returned. He called out for me: "Miss? Miss? Are you there?"

"Yes," I replied anxiously.

"Shine your light, and wave it around," he commanded. I did as instructed. Within minutes, he was at the front edge of my roof. "Where are you?" he asked. "I am at the back," I answered.

I heard muffled footsteps, and suddenly he was standing alongside me. He noticed my cane. "Can you stand?" he inquired.

"Yes," I answered, "but I'll need a little help." And help me he did. Moreover, with a little coaxing and additional help from the other male passenger in the boat, I was able to depart my roof and board the small craft. Once I was in the boat, we all introduced ourselves; my rescuer's name was Paul, and this was his recreational dinghy. The other man was Alton. Paul had chosen to survey the neighborhood in his boat after the storm, looking for stranded victims.

I was so overwhelmed by Paul's apparent acts of kindness that I repeatedly thanked him. But he was adamant; Paul shook his head no. "I am just letting the Lord use me," he replied. "This storm is just as frightening to me as it is for everyone." He and Alton continued rowing the boat.

Nervously, I began asking a million questions. "Where are we going? Is the whole city flooded? Will they let us in at the Superdome? Are the helicopters going to pick us up?"

But again the Samaritan hushed me. "Miss, I really don't have many answers for you. Right now, I am going to bring you to my place. I have food, lights, and water. You can rest there for the night, and we'll figure out something by morning."

His answers were reasonable, but somehow I found no solace in them. In fact, new anxieties began to arise. It suddenly dawned on me that I was in a boat navigated by two male strangers and I had no idea of our destination. Although I considered Paul a Samaritan for his good deeds, who was he really? And where was his home? And what made it safe? Why wasn't it flooded? I froze as I felt chills creep up my spine.

What had I done? Who were these people? What was going to happen to me? I was fearful, but I decided to feign conviction as I further interrogated my rescuers. "Where is your house?" I quizzed. "How come you have lights? Why can't we just go to the Superdome?" I asked.

Sensing my apprehension, the men began to laugh, which frightened me more. "My house is just up here to your right," Paul offered. I peered to my right. I did not see anything but the outline of darkened homes.

"I thought you said you had lights," I challenged.

"Yes, I do," he said. He interrupted my next barrage of questions by assuring me that he not only had lights, but also a generator. Moreover, he explained that there were other people at his home, so I should relax. "I know what you may be thinking, Ms. Jane, but if you trust the Lord, then just bear with me a little while longer," he urged.

CHAPTER 10

Well, there it was in a nutshell. I needed to hold on to something. And what he said made some sense. I'd professed having trust in God, and certainly there was little or nothing more I could do. So I just sat there, gripping my possessions and silently praying while attempting to appear trusting. Lo and behold, we finally arrived at a location where both men rapidly got out of the boat. The water was knee deep. They began pulling and pushing the canoe with great effort toward an unlit home. Nervousness plagued my soul. I could not speak. I mentally started recalling the words to the 23rd Psalm.

"Ms. Jane," Paul was saying, "give me your hand." I started to protest, but then I decided against it. As I was being assisted out of the boat, Alton walked over to the unlit house and opened the front door. I peered inside; it was dark. As I waded hesitantly toward the door, my night vision adjusted. I was able to make out figures. My ears picked up sounds.

Paul asked, "Hey, what happened to my lights?"

Someone responded, "The generator kicked off."

"So y'all are just sitting in the dark?" Paul questioned.

"Yeah, we figured you'd be back before long," someone answered.

"This here is Ms. Jane," Paul introduced me. "She is kind of scared. Give her a place to sit while I go check on the generator," he instructed.

CHAPTER 11

The next thing I knew, I was sitting in a dark room filled with people—women, men, and children—and, from the few distinguishable muffled barks, at least one dog. It took a few minutes, but the lights were restored, and Paul was once again in our midst. We introduced ourselves and anxiously discussed the events at hand. I was mesmerized by the details. It seemed that New Orleans had been declared a disaster area; our city was 80 percent underwater. My thoughts were jumbled as I tried to make sense of this new information. If the hurricane was no longer a threat, then what was making the water rise?

I was surrounded by a family of six: a grandmother (Ms. Dee), her two grown daughters (Marge and Helen), and Marge's two teenage sons (Lance and Curtis). Helen's fiancé was also a part of their group. It was Alton, the man who'd accompanied Paul during my rescue. In addition to this family, there was a middle-aged neighbor man, Eugene; a self-proclaimed preacher who preferred to be addressed as "Rev"; a senior couple, Mr. and Mrs. Bergeron; and their toy poodle, Misty.

"It's the same thing as with Betsy," Ms. Dee explained. "They are mixing business with politics. Ain't nobody worried about us. When them folk that's in charge realized that this city was risking 100 percent flooding, the first thing that come to their minds are the levees."

"Yeah," Eugene added, bluntly. "When it comes to neighborhoods versus city finance or profits, there can only be one winner."

Alton and Paul also agreed. "You see, Ms. Jane," Paul advised, "it's a matter of money. New Orleans is all about tourism and business. If we lose those markets, this city will be in a world of hurt. So naturally you have to know the powers that be had a lot to do with these present conditions."

"Sure, we are 80 percent flooded, but you can bet the 20 percent that's dry is up there around the business district," Alton predicted.

"You are not saying …" I hesitated. "Our levees were purposely breached?"

"Breached, compromised, bombed!" Rev exclaimed excitedly, his eyes bulging.

"Uh-huh," Marge and Helen concurred in unison.

"I know you heard that huge boom earlier today?" Helen asked. I nodded. "Well, that was just the tip of the iceberg. It seems a barge got loose and found its way downriver, where it inevitably rammed into levee walls. The Corps of Engineers are saying that the impact of the barge against the levee caused stress fractures, which eventually weakened the structure and which in turn put this whole city at risk," she concluded.

"That's right," Marge counseled. "We've been monitoring media coverage since we got here. There are rampant inferences and lots of allegations, but no solid proof. Nonetheless, at least three sections of the levees have been damaged. Water is seeping in from everywhere—the canals, the lake, and the Mississippi. Moreover, and without doubt, our city is under siege, underwater, and under martial law."

"So what will happen to us?" I quavered, sounding very much like a small child. "What are we supposed to do?" But this time, there were no answers. Paul tried to get us to eat something, but we were too hyped. We chattered nervously the rest of the night and monitored the news programs, hoping to pick up useful information.

And although I wasn't sure of what lay ahead, I was still grateful for God's protection. I silently thanked Him and prayed for an end to this nightmare.

CHAPTER 12

The next day was Tuesday, August 30, 2005. We awakened to sputtering, mechanical choking sounds—the generator had stopped again. This time, Paul could not revive it. Thus, the water began invading his home. A decision was made. We could not stay there. Paul thought it would be safer if we moved to higher ground. He said he had earlier scouted the area and found the streets closer to the highway to be drier. He recommended that we band together and wade toward Highway 90. He felt confident that the helicopters or some officials would have easier access to us if we were at a higher level. We begged him to come with us, but he refused, stating that God was not finished with him. He wanted to resume looking for others who might be stranded. Thus, we bade him farewell and commenced our journey to safety.

Our first stop was Chef Menteur Highway 90, and it was indeed dry. In fact, coming from our subdivision and now standing in an area seemingly unaffected by the storm seemed weird. Yet we were unscathed and prepared; at least we thought we were. There were twelve of us: the matriarch, her two grown daughters, the two grandsons, the boyfriend, the senior couple and their toy poodle, the self-proclaimed minister, the middle-aged gentleman, and me. We struck an agreement and made a pact. We decided to stay together and protect each other as best we could while endeavoring to escape the rising waters and whatever else that lay ahead.

This pact, however, did not last very long. I believe we had good intentions, but there were just too many temptations, which eventually demolished our objectives. The first thing that defeated our goodwill was finding out that the city was wide open. We were in a situation where it appeared that placing undue emphasis on self-sustainment was top priority. While at the interstate awaiting rescue, we witnessed widespread looting and small-scale rioting. When we were able to flag down police cruisers or fire trucks, we were told by the officials that there was nothing they could do. We were advised to just hold tight until rescuers could get to us. When we asked about food and water, we were told, "When in Rome, do as the Romans do"—in other words, to go into the stores and get what was needed. And we did.

At first, timid and guilt-ridden, we attempted to put together a verbal list of items: rubbing alcohol, insect repellent, hand sanitizers, juice, water, canned meats, toilet paper, etc. After a while, the men in our group would depart on their own and return with other items: batteries, shoes, T-shirts, towels, and so on. The women acted as judges; we challenged each item as it was presented. "Now, y'all know we don't need that," we would chide. "Y'all need to put that back. We are not thieves," we reminded when presented items that did not meet basic needs. But no amount of chiding or reprimand could prevent the inevitable. Eugene, the neighbor man, became totally intrigued with the idea of commandeering free-flowing assets. He no longer sought approval for his acquired property but rather was more interested in finding storage space.

CHAPTER 13

Nonetheless, as dusk approached, the proposition of remaining on the street became less desirous. We were concerned for our safety and equally fearful of contracting the West Nile virus. A couple of the males in our group decided to seek help from a nearby religious facility; however, this effort failed as well. The men returned only to tell us that the seminary refused to help. The officials at the school were afraid that with all the looting and chaos, they would be inviting trouble if they opened their doors to us.

However, there was some good news! After the men were rejected by the facility, one of the theology instructors privately divulged useful information to our guys. He advised that if we somehow could move to a proper rescue site, rather than wait for pickup, we'd stand a better chance. Moreover, the nearest rescue location in our area was supplied. We didn't need a vote to decipher our next move. We were looking for a way out, and it had been given to us. We did not hesitate, plan, or dally. Although we moved as a group, individual effort was mandatory. We were fatigued, hungry, and haggard, yet we left the dry highway and headed back toward water-engorged streets.

We treaded water as if our very lives were in danger. But here, too, was where we began to disband. For the middle-aged man, Eugene, had become hooked by the lured of ill-gotten gain; he did not follow us toward rescue but chose instead to remain with his illegal cache. By the time we arrived at the rescue point, we were minus one man and one dog; Mr. and Mrs. Bergeron's poodle had not survived the hazardous trek.

I am not sure how long Misty had been part of the Bergeron family, but their response to his death was truly moving. We wanted to express sympathy or offer condolences for their loss, but we were caught in an awkward moment. We arrived at the site and immediately were put into boats. So much was going on and being said that it was mass confusion. But without hesitation or remorse, Mrs. B just handed Misty over to one of the volunteers. As the boat was paddled toward the interstate, the senior couple sat silently holding hands and staring ahead toward the future.

CHAPTER 14

Once on the interstate, we were allowed to disembark. We were told to wait there until trucks came to pick us up. We went to join the hundreds of others who were already waiting. We asked questions and were told that freight, furniture, and army trucks were being used to take people to the Superdome or the Convention Center. The trucks had been coming and going all day, but it appeared that as night approached, the trucks had slowed their pickup times. The people on the interstate were becoming restless. Everyone was pushing forward, vying for better positions in the poorly formed line. About an hour later, and after two other boats had delivered more people, a truck finally came. The crowd made a mad dash toward it. The driver was yelling, "Let the elderly and disabled get on first." But the crowd was not hearing that nonsense. Whoever could get on, got on. And no one was about to get off. So after assuring the remaining crowd that other trucks were coming, the driver drove off.

Another hour or more passed. Two trucks came. Again, people ran riotously toward the trucks. This time, however, one driver did not open his doors. He allowed the majority of the crowd to board the first truck before making his announcement: "This truck is for the disabled, the sick, and the elderly. There will probably be room for others, but right now, I am only allowing these categories of people to board." With that being said, two healthy young men along with the driver begin assisting people who required help to board the truck. I was impressed—so much so that I turned to inform my group that I was going to board that truck. But with all the mayhem surrounding us, my announcement was lost in the delivery. Needless to say, once in the truck, I discovered that I was no longer part of the pact. Nonetheless, I reasoned, since all the trucks were heading in the same direction, I'd probably be reunited.

CHAPTER 15

I was riding in a dark truck, surrounded by people with an array of maladies. Besides crutches, portable oxygen tanks, canes, and wheelchairs, there were individuals exhibiting signs of dementia. Depression was quite visible, too, but so was optimism. We were all talking incessantly—to each other, to ourselves, and shouting to the driver. We were just glad to be getting away!

About forty minutes later, the truck stopped. The young men and the driver began assisting us out of the truck. I was not out yet, but I heard someone complain, "This ain't the Superdome. I thought you were bringing us to the Superdome."

I heard the driver answer, "The Dome is full. I was instructed to bring y'all here." When I got to the exit of the truck, I was helped out. I realized with naive relief that we were at the Convention Center. True, at first I had wanted to go to the Dome, but after careful thought, I figured the Convention Center would be better. After all, the Dome had been opened prior to the storm for evacuees, and if more victims had been taken there after the storm, then it was probably full to capacity. I figured they must have just recently opened the Convention Center; therefore, it would be more accommodating and less crowded.

I entered the Center only to discover I was wrong again! There were walls and walls of people. The Center was evidently being run on a generator. It had limited lights and no food, drinking water, or other basic necessities. It had low water pressure, so the toilets were unappealingly odorous and stagnated. As I walked around, looking for a vacant area to rest, I spied members of my group. They seemed to have acquired an area for themselves and were deep into conversation. Of course, when I spotted them, I felt some relief. I sauntered over to their area and once again became a member of the fold.

They filled me in on the latest bulletins. It seemed that the National Guard had been activated to help with evacuation efforts as well as to arrest and detain looters. There were also reports of confusion among President Bush, FEMA Director Brown, Louisiana Governor Blanco, and New Orleans Mayor Nagin as to whom would be responsible for rescuing and evacuating the citizens who were now stuck at the Superdome or left behind in their flooded homes. "What about the Convention Center? Why aren't they mentioning the Convention Center?" I asked; however, no response was offered. So I secretly prayed and convinced myself that every time they mentioned the Superdome, officials were including the evacuees at the Convention Center as well.

CHAPTER 16

Again I was wrong. We stayed at the Convention Center a total of four infinite days and equally disturbing nights. It wasn't until the third day that, miraculously, the media broke the story that besides the thousands of people in the Dome who needed rescue, there were also throngs of evacuees at the Convention Center. Moreover, my stay at the Convention Center was severely marred by thug mentalities, self-appointed leaders, horror stories, unsanitary conditions, and stifling hot weather. For the most part, one might attribute these impairments to my state of mind, for indeed I was in denial and could not always determine reality from fallacy. To me, the Convention Center's atmosphere was hallucinogenic; there are no terms to describe the feeling of desperation and abandonment. I watched the looters become heroes, thugs incite riots, and the people become aimless. Further, I was inundated by countless rumors of rapes, murders, and torture. It didn't take long before apathy set in. You just somehow knew that in order to survive this arena, you needed thicker skin. And consequently, it did not take long before insensitivity, true to form, disrupted and deteriorated the moral conscientiousness of even people with the best intentions.

The one hundred hours I spent at the Convention Center seemed like an eternity. Due to sweltering temperatures, congested space, and health risks, we were constantly on the move, drifting from one area to the next, trying to avoid the heat, filth, and corruption. I am not sure about the others, but my mind, too, was adrift. Mental images unfurled before me. I inscribed imaginary notes between reels. Nonetheless, my attempts to blot out the ugliness of the Center failed. On one such occasion, as I endeavored to eradicate my surroundings, a distinct voice and image from my past accosted me. Initially, and because my thoughts were muddled, I could not determine if I was hallucinating or experiencing reality.

There was a lady with very pale skin, piercing dark eyes, and coal-black hair. She stood in the middle of the street and screeched violently. Her words and sentences rambled. Her arms flailed nervously; her movement and directions were erratic. I'd seen this lady once before. About six weeks prior to the storm, I'd had an appointment with my orthopedic surgeon. I needed to pick up paperwork to present my employer concerning my physical constraints. When I got to the doctor's office, there was no one in the waiting area; that is, no one except this woman—this same woman who now stood on Convention Boulevard. She emulated the same screeching noise and flailing movements that she had exhibited during our first encounter.

CHAPTER 17

Six weeks ago, however, upon seeing her, I was frightened. I wondered why no one was trying to help her. The workers at the doctor's office were staring at the woman from behind the glass window of the receptionist's area. When I reached the window and requested my paperwork, no one said anything to me about the woman. I received my documents and swiftly departed the office. As I left, the sound of her voice seemed to follow me. I did not know what to think or what to do. I just sped up my escape. But once in my car, I suffered humanitarian remorse. Was there something I should or could have done?

But I eased my conscience by justifying logically that this woman needed professional help; help that I certainly could not provide. I concluded that since she was in a medical facility, no doubt officials had been called, and she would receive the proper care. With this logic firmly intact, I happily dismissed the woman from my world. But now, here at the Convention Center and amongst the ruthlessness and mayhem, she had resurfaced. Immediately I was plagued with guilt. Her words and actions were still confusing, but somehow, I likened her to John the Baptist—eccentric yet ominous. Perhaps this was God's messenger. But if so, her words were nonetheless incomprehensible. I watched intently as she babbled and walked back and forth. Over time, I noticed that there were actual lucid moments during her tirades. At these times, her eyes became softer, her movements lessened, and her speech muted. During these silences, she appeared less threatening and more approachable. I decided to attempt amends; I waited for the precise moment.

When her eyes softened and her voice paused, I pursued her. "Miss, Miss," I said, beckoning. "Do you want a place to sit?" She stared in my direction. I pointed to the empty chair next to me. "Why don't you come sit a while?" I coached. She continued to stare. Her eyes finally focused, and we connected. "It sure is hot," I added. But she did not respond. I pointed again to the vacant chair. "If you want," I continued, "you can sit here." She did not move. "Don't be scared," I assured her. "We are not going to hurt you," I promised. "Come on," I begged, "sit with us." She remained motionless. I was beginning to feel a little foolish. It was evident that this woman did not understand me. Moreover, I could hear some snickering from the people in the immediate area. I did not know if the ridicule included people in my group or if it was random consensus. Nonetheless, there was no time to address the hecklers, for at that moment, a huge uproar commenced. Someone screamed, "The water is coming!"

CHAPTER 18

Oh, no! I thought. *Not that nonsense again.* We'd been at the Center for days, and the information that the water was coming was certainly not news. In fact, within hours of our arrival at the Convention Center, we were introduced to this foolishness. Actually, it was more of a scam. Somehow, thug mentality had created an infallible heist to separate people from their property. They preyed upon the fear created by floodwater. They knew that people were severely distraught by the water that had driven them from their homes. The criminals obviously figured that recreating the same fear would stimulate chaos and thereby provide them with illegal gains. Upon hearing the verbal alarm that the water was coming, thousands of people would run aimlessly, abandoning personal property in their wake. And of course, if and when they regained composure, they'd discover that not only had they been tricked, but what little possession they'd previously owned had now disappeared.

I was lucky; more than half the members of my group, for various reasons, were unable to walk quickly. When we first heard the threatening cry, we were frantic. If this alarm was true, we would be in big trouble. For that reason, during our first exposure to the disruption following the "water" alarm, we decided to seek a higher level. Although it meant climbing stairs, it was better than trying to maneuver at high speeds though mass hysteria. When we got to the second floor of the Convention Center, we gained entry to one of the meeting rooms. While there, we met others who had chosen this more practical escape rather than risk a stampede.

These people educated us and calmed our fears. The water, they explained, was not coming; at least it had not come in all the time they'd been at the Center. They advised us that it was a scam. And as time went on, and the alarm became more frequent, we, too, ascertained that it was indeed a cruel and calculative hoax.

But just then, as I was waiting for some positive response from the mystery woman, the fictitious alarm was absolutely exasperating. As the cry went out, mass confusion ensued. There were still people very much affected by the prospect of floodwater. They ran amok into the streets, crashing and stumbling into anyone and anything that stood in their way. My group was unmoved, along with many others. Instead, we huddled together defiantly. "There's no water!" we countered. "No water is coming!" we yelled. Perceivably, within slow-motion minutes, our area became calm. Those who believed the hype were gone, and we who remained were unharmed. We were grateful for God's protection.

We watched in quiet awe as people returned. They picked through abandoned property, trying to relocate their belongings and prior positions. Actually, the people returning could have been the thieves who'd orchestrated this fiasco, for there was no way of discerning who or what belonged together. In the midst of these matters, I became painfully aware that the mystery woman had also disappeared. She, no doubt, had been swept away by the foolishness. I was instantly sad; my attempt at atonement had been sabotaged. Nonetheless, I rationalized that I could not grieve missed opportunities—especially now. My whole voyage thus far had been upon a vessel of misguidance. Miraculously, I found inner strength and vowed an end to ghost chasing, looking for fault, or assigning blame. This, after all, was an "act of God." What I needed instead was reassessment. Atonement, if I truly desired it, should commence in a more realistic arena. The callous atmosphere of the Convention Center had diluted the camaraderie our group once shared. In particular, Alton seemed the one most changed.

CHAPTER 19

Alton, I suppose due to his agility and eagerness to provide the group with food, had assigned himself a new role. He apparently mistook our appreciation for indebtedness and thereby appointed himself ruler. His first clandestine act had been to oust Rev from the group. I guess the reason may have been linked to the two of them constantly butting heads over most issues, but more likely it was a "man thing": there could be only one leader. Likewise, I and the Bergerons were also targeted by Alton. If we did not agree with his plans or if we challenged his ideas, then, surprisingly, there would be less food to go around. Nonetheless, this did not prevent us from challenging him. And each time Alton endeavored to exile us, the Bergerons, myself, and sometimes even Ms. Dee would inevitably disrupt his attempts. This infuriated Alton. Although he did not vocalize his disappointments, he would nonetheless twist his face to such a degree that you'd think he was experiencing seizures. As humorous as this was to watch, I made genuine efforts to end my debates with him. After all, although my state of shock kept me from craving nourishment, Alton's resourcefulness was a great asset for the group. It took tremendous restraint on my part, but by God's grace, I managed to allow Alton his allotted minutes of fame. Unfortunately, having lived most of my life on my own recognizance, I knew this concession would be short-lived.

During our next impromptu meeting, I announced my decision to depart the group. We had been informed that buses were coming to evacuate us the next morning, Saturday, September 3, 2005.

Alton had been pressuring us to walk from one end of Convention Boulevard to the other so that we could have our pick of conveyances. I wasn't sure if he was being astute, cunning, or downright mean, but I knew that the distance was beyond my ability. Logically I objected; I reminded him that city officials had instructed that we were to simply board the buses without opposition.

CHAPTER 20

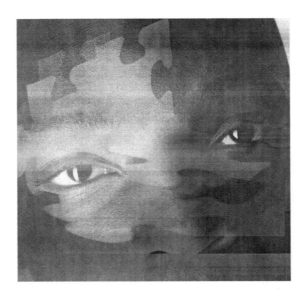

But Alton was certain that we could improve our chances of survival if we chose our own destination. I told him that having gone through this whole ordeal, my only desire was to get out of New Orleans. I did not have a state or any particular city in mind. I just wanted to feel human again and achieve some form of normalcy. The group was torn, but I held my position; I persuaded them to go on without me. "I believe in God," I said. "He has brought me thus far, and I intend to lean on Him all the way," I concluded. I knew that they did not have much choice. It was either stay with me or continue with Alton. And thus far, Alton had been the hand that provided them with food.

So as a party of one, that Saturday afternoon, when the buses arrived to evacuate us, I departed the Convention Center. I did not ask questions; I did not demand answers; I simply boarded a bus and prayed for deliverance. As the bus headed toward the airfield, I peered out of the windows, staring at the remnants of my home town. My world was upside down, my body ached, and I formulated my thoughts haphazardly. I sat there transfixed, glad to be alive, and wondering what would happen next! I was hungry, needed water, and desired sleep! But, by far, I desperately wanted to regain purpose and self-reliance.

The bus arrived at the airfield, and we boarded huge helicopters. The noise was deafening. The propellers whirled and spun, creating astronomical wind blasts and earth-shattering noises. But it did not matter. We were no longer the forgotten masses. We were being rescued! I was strapped into my seat, and within minutes the copter began to rise. It was as though a cumbersome weight had been lifted from my shoulder. Immediately I began to seek slumber as refuge.

CHAPTER 21

My salvation was short-lived. It appeared that only minutes had lapsed before the helicopter was once again on the ground. I was confused. How long had I been out? Where were we? I was looking out of the windows, trying to get a fix on our location. The copter spun to a halt, and we were told to exit. Someone guided us to a chain-link fence, and we were told to enter the gates and get in line. We did. Minutes later, we found ourselves in a seemingly endless line that snaked and curled its way to nowhere. We passed numerous buildings, doorways, parking spaces, stairwells, and more, but the line continued. As the line crept up, we did, too. We noticed guardsmen, police officers, and perhaps airport workers from time to time, walking nearby. We addressed questions to them but got no response. Minutes turned into hours and hours into half a day. We were still in line, inching, circling, and edging our way toward the unknown. I didn't see food, but there was bottled water along our path, and occasionally someone left the line to get a drink. I passed on the water; I didn't want to jeopardize my position in line.

Sunlight disappeared, and evening shadows began to dominate our surroundings. The line moved up another few feet, and with some relief, we saw a doorway in the distance that seemed to be the end of the line. We also noticed, with some dismay, that the line was no longer a single entity.

There were now two lines adjacent to each another. *Where did these people come from?* I was thinking. *Were they here already?* But I had no time for answers, for I noticed the line I was in beginning to tighten. It was as though the people felt threatened. They began to close in vacant spaces between themselves and the people ahead of them. I, too, closed in my area. The promised door loomed in front of us, and although we were still quite a distance away, we could see people being allowed inside. But the magic line had once again multiplied. There were now three lines weaving their way toward the mystery door. It was at this point that I could no longer stave off my existing aches and pains. My hips, thighs, and calves were severely sore, cramped, and burning. I was praying, "God, please give me strength," for I knew I had to endure standing in line. I was holding onto my cane with two hands; the straps of my overnight bag were uncomfortably slung across my neck while the bag, itself, bounced irritably against my back. I methodically dragged myself forward. By the time we got within a few feet of the treasured doorway, the lines dissipated, and in their place was a mob. People began yelling, pushing, and shoving. I stood aloof but did not yield my position.

CHAPTER 22

Several policemen came out to subdue the unruly crowd. They threatened to close the entryway and to send rioters to the end of the line. At any other time, these threats might have worked. But we were in the midst of a disaster, and the crowd, by far, outnumbered the police officers. Hecklers within the crowd shouted obscenities and continued to push forward. The officers retreated into the building and closed the door behind them. Ten minutes later, the door reopened; the officers reiterated their previous threats. This time the crowd, although unrelenting, was less rowdy. About a dozen people were allowed admittance. This procedure went on for some time, with twelve people entering and a waiting period of approximately twenty minutes between each entry. This was acceptable, considering the circumstances; however, considering my deteriorating mobility, it was torturous. Nonetheless, I kept moving. Just about then, I heard the magical words that virtually saved my life: "Tower of Power." In the midst of total chaos, someone was standing near the coveted doorway chanting the name "Tower of Power." I had no idea of its origin or why it was being touted. My gazed was fixed upon the prized door. The guy to my rear nudged me.

"Miss," he said, "you need to go over there." —He motioned toward the mysterious "Tower of Power" chanter.

"Why would I want to go there?" I asked blandly, trying to disguise my annoyance.

"They can help you," he informed me. I stared at him quizzically. He pointed to my cane. "You are handicapped, right?"

I thought about his question momentarily. "No," I finally answered. "I just had surgery," I explained.

"It doesn't matter," he said, interrupting me. "You ain't going make it in this line. If I was you, I'd go there," he said, again nodding in the chanter's direction.

I stared at him, keenly studying his face and then his logic. "I … I don't know," I stuttered. "I don't want any trouble. I just …"

"Miss," he, dryly, interjected, "Go get in their line."

Against my better judgment, but because my pain had taken complete charge, I crossed over into the handicapped line. I felt badly and was riddled with guilt. I worried that my temporary impairment would not be enough to qualify me as a Tower of Power recipient. I feared rejection or being made to return to the previous line. Nonetheless, I gathered my courage and held my position. I eased my pangs of guilt with quiet prayers and remembering that God provides.

"Welcome," the chanter greeted me. "Go on in, sister. Someone will assist you," he told me. I turned to wave at my benefactor, but he had mysteriously disappeared into the crowd. I was now inside the building. There, in front of me, was an escalator. It was not working, but I was being beckoned forward.

"You need help?" someone asked.

I shook my head. I held onto my cane and overnight bag with one hand, grabbed onto the escalator's rail with the other, and proceeded upward. When I got to the second landing, someone called out, "Tower of Power," and I noticed a small group of people standing together. I was motioned over.

"Don't be afraid," the leader said. "We know you have suffered much, but know also that God has not forsaken you." His voice and his message were the exact prescription I needed to calm my fears. After a few additional words of encouragement, he led us in a prayer. Moreover, before departing, he wished us a safe and spiritual journey.

CHAPTER 23

Next, a lady came over with a clipboard and asked for names, addresses and Social Security numbers; I gave my information. She inscribed the data onto her log and motioned us toward an area of cushioned chairs. We were told to wait there until we were called for boarding. We waited. An hour later, we commenced boarding a C-130. Having retired military status, I recognized this as a military carrier. As we boarded, we were given MRE (Meals Ready to Eat) packets. Again, having served in the military and having eaten these meals on many occasions, I was familiar with their contents, yet I declined. It was not that the food wasn't good, but rather that it was too cumbersome. As my life up until this point had been twisted enough, I did not want any other complexities. When the craft began to taxi the runway, I double-checked my safety belt and settled back for some serious sleep. I closed my eyes and let my tension, aches, and worries fade into oblivion. And for a few solitary moments, I was actually content. *This could all be a dream*, I told myself. And if it weren't for the loud engine of the carrier and the yelling voices of passengers as they struggled to make themselves heard, I might have been able to believe that.

At about 7:30 PM on Sunday, September 4, 2005, the pilot announced that we would be landing at Fort Smith, Arkansas, in approximately twenty minutes. *Arkansas*. I pondered. I had never been to Arkansas. I had heard of it and knew some of its history; I had no problem locating in on a map. Yet, I was skeptical, "We are in Arkansas?" I mused.

CHAPTER 24

We landed and found buses waiting. We got onto the buses and were taken to Fort Chaffee, Arkansas. Once there, we got off the buses and were housed in military barracks. The wooden structures were old but nonetheless accommodating. The beds were metal frames with single mattresses and coil springs; there were also opened-bay showers with lots of hot water, and flushable commodes. The bunks had clean linen, and the bathrooms contained fresh towels, Further, the buildings contained toiletries, storage lockers, indoor water coolers, and air conditioning. It was not the Ritz, but I rated it better then the Convention Center. We spent the night there.

The next morning was Labor Day, Monday, September 5, 2005. I awakened to the delicious, wafting aroma of bacon and eggs. I endeavored to stand, but I found that my legs were still weak. I sat at the edge of my bed and watched as several people passed me with foil-covered trays. Hunger overcame my natural shyness around strangers. "They are serving food?" I asked.

"Sure are," one of the food carriers answered.

"Where?" I stammered.

"In what they say is the mess hall," someone answered. "It's a couple of streets up the road and a few more toward the right."

"Is there transportation?" I inquired. I was informed that there was a bus that would pick you up if you were standing at the stop. I grimaced. I knew that I would not be able to transport myself to the bus stop, let alone to the mess hall. So I laid back in my bunk. I reasoned that more rest would later afford me the strength needed to support mobility.

When I awoke again, I noted that it was nearly 4:30 PM. I surmised that I'd probably missed lunch. I wondered if my legs had regained some strength. I stood and walked back and forth briefly. There was some discomfort but a relatively low amount of pain. I began my journey toward the door, but I was halted momentarily as a slew of people rushed in, passing me swiftly. "What's up?" I inquired.

"The buses are coming," I was told.

"What buses?" I asked. It was then explained that buses were coming to transport us to another location. Reportedly, the actual number of evacuees had been more than calculated. It had been decided to move us in order to make room for other victims. Thus, my planned meal was once again put on hold. I returned to my bunk and gathered my belongings. I hobbled down the porch steps and stood along the street with the others. Soldiers came by with boxes of meal packets and issued them to us. This time, without hesitation, I gladly accepted the packet.

The buses arrived roughly two hours later, and we boarded. Once seated, I eagerly devoured and enjoyed my issued meal. We arrived at a camping facility—complete with cabins, a fishing pond, and picnic areas—at around midnight on Tuesday, September 6, 2005. The shelter, located in Saline County, was actually a mountain retreat for youngsters. The town's population, we later learned, was less than two hundred. We, on the other hand, totaled more than five hundred!

CHAPTER 25

When we got off the buses, we were greeted by a sea of white faces—some friendly, some indifferent, but the majority stern. We were advised that bedding, clean towels, toiletries, hot meals, and showers awaited us. Prior to the provision of these comforts, the camp director and counselors attempted to register and process us. This indeed was understandable; however, it was the manner and the verbal tone they utilized that I didn't appreciate. Although we were better off, we were still numb from our aforementioned afflictions. We expected compassion and empathy, but instead we were greeted by perversity.

The director, wearing denim overalls and using a bullhorn, yelled instructions. And some of the counselors seemed visibly irritated when we weren't able to provide requested information. "Listen up, people," the director yelled. "Y'all ain't in New Orleans. This here is Arkansas." We were offended by their callous inference.

We expressed our discontent: "This may not be New Orleans, but we are not children, either. Can't this nonsense wait till morning?" Our defiance surprised them. Surely they were expecting a more humbled, defeated group—people willing to compromise. But we, instead, were obstinate. We'd lost everything, but we would not submit to conformity. On the other hand, some, like me, were too tired to argue. We understood the need to record information, but we still weren't receptive to the bullhorn or the irrational behavior. After several attempts to restore order, the director finally relented and signaled for the commencement of bed assignments. This whole incident seemed horribly archaic. The mood and attitudes, without a doubt, raised serious undertones of racism. Undoubtedly, the camp was supposedly helping us, but why was it necessary to attempt forced submissiveness?

CHAPTER 26

As time went on, the acts of inequity slowly overshadowed what at first had appeared to be good intent. For example, when we went through the meal lines, we were given unbelievably small portions of food. We were stunned, and appropriately we requested more. But the response was, "No, eat what is given. If you want more, return to the end of the line. And if there is extra, it will be rationed at that time." Although this sounds fair, it was horrible. Why would you volunteer to shelter survivors who hadn't eaten or slept in days, and the first thing you do is to ration nourishment? But once more, I was indebted to God's wisdom. For though my body was in such pain, mind games could not overtake me. Accordingly, I was accepting and humble.

So this is Arkansas! I thought. *It certainly hasn't changed much over the years.* As best I could piece together, Arkansas had won notoriety in the late 1950s for trying to block integration at one of its high schools. It also achieved historic distinction for being one of the last states to sanction civil rights. Although I was glad to be out of New Orleans, I began to question the true depth of my good fortune. It did not take long to deduce that subtle discrimination was cunningly afoot. Having lived in the South all of my life, I was well familiar with Jim Crow politics, but it had been years since I'd been subjected to segregation ploys. And this summation was not just attained from the early treatment we received. For in the days that followed, as we were allowed to venture into the communities and interact with other citizens, we began to sense an overall injustice. People would frown at us without reason, purposely avoid eye contact, and attempt to correct our speech, or merely ignore our presence. Our mood quickly changed to match the arena in which we found ourselves. We were angered, and we felt betrayed. We wanted safety but were not willing to compromise our dignity in exchange for comfort.

Once phone lines were made available at the camp and we had opportunity to contact friends and family, many evacuees who had relatives living in other states chose to leave. They might not have had a choice concerning their arrival in Arkansas, but they now had the option to leave. And many opted to seek refuge elsewhere, gladly teasing and hazing the less fortunate, such as me, as they departed. "Y'all better be careful out here in these woods. Y'all might outnumber the town folks, but there are certainly enough trees to make up the difference." I took their taunts good-naturedly, because that was exactly what they were. They were getting out, and we were staying behind. Still, I did not let their scoffing bother me. Arkansas, although different from New Orleans, was a safe location. And even though I did not understand or accept the subtle insults directed at us, I did not fear for my life. In essence, my prayers had been answered: I wasn't waterlogged, surrounded by venomous mosquitoes, or at the mercy of thugs, thieves, or self-imposed rulers. Moreover, I had a clean bed; hot showers, clean clothes, and adequate nourishment. I didn't need a pity party. What I needed was constructive planning—ways to regroup, get my game on, and find a way out of this nightmare!

CHAPTER 27

The camp remained operational for approximately six weeks; they were supposed to stay open longer, but as more of us opted to leave, it became a less profitable arrangement. But in those six weeks, the belittling continued unabated, for although the bullhorn disappeared, the attitude of supremacy remained. The camp director and several staffers attempted in many ways to herd and berate us. They tried unsuccessfully to reshape our method of communication. They thought it would be more effective if we'd wait until being addressed before offering opinions, asking questions, or making comments. They further implied that we were irresponsible, disrespectful, and lazy. Some openly mocked our accents and threatened to remove us from the shelter if we did not comply with their policies. Nonetheless, we who remained managed to persevere without serious incident. It became accepted knowledge that we needed these innkeepers as much as they needed us. The shelter was being funded by FEMA. We learned that this was just one of the many facilities volunteering shelter in exchange for federal funds. The camp had the contacts and vouchers needed in order for us to move on. So rather than get into a whizzing contest, we maintained level heads. Oh, sure, at night in our assigned bunks, we'd discuss and even laugh at our benefactors. But truth be known, we recognized that although pulling different loads, we were yoked together.

As such, I had to disentangle the web of confusion that entrapped me. I had to push aside the barricade that corrupted my judgment, obscured my vision, and blocked my blessings. Arkansas might have been a culture of smoldering racial imbalance, but it was nevertheless my temporary solace. I had to look beyond the obvious differences and seek wholeheartedly the means in which to make this place more palatable. Nothing is—with the exception of God's love—ever all good or, for that matter, all bad. I had willingly fled New Orleans after Katrina in search of safety. I'd fought long and hard during my flight to keep my dignity. And now that I'd achieved half the battle, I wasn't about to get turned around. I could not allow archaic concepts to derail my mission. Arkansas, a spacious tree-lined milieu, held a lot of quaint charms. I liked the widespread and quiet communities, the family-oriented activities, the overall cleanliness (both on highways and in inner cities), the numerous shopping malls, and the low crime rate. I was mesmerized by the mountainous terrain and the ample woods, parks, picnic areas, and campgrounds. This place, with the exception of some racial discord, was beautiful!

Having come from New Orleans, a city highly noted for elevated crime statistics, and having survived Hurricane Katrina, I surmised that life is never perfect. Sure, I'd achieved moderate comfort in New Orleans, and while living there, I'd considered my life to be reasonably cozy. But the calm I'd achieved there was partially due to my ability to tune out the negative and immerse myself in the positive, such as parades, music, Super Bowl games, Creole and Cajun cuisine, riverboats, local festivals, the pride of having a National League football team, and the love of family and friends. Moreover, I decided that in the many years that God had blessed me on this

Earth, nothing had ever been effortless. If I could make it in New Orleans, then surely I could survive Arkansas.

CHAPTER 28

As I learned to let go of self-righteousness and relinquish some of my anger, I began to appreciate the natural beauty that surrounded me. Moreover, I discovered that not everyone at the camp were conspirators, for in the midst of us were angels! Perhaps they'd been there all along; but in my attempts to block racism, I'd suffered impaired vision. These magnificent men and women from the surrounding communities had volunteered to work at the camp. They came daily and would assist with staff duties, but as time went on and as their help became less required, they instead began to offer personal services to us. They ran errands, provided transportation, invited us to dine, brought clothing, or just sat and talked. They were friendly, caring, and quality people. Their good deeds were not questionable. They gave of their time and selves freely. Their camaraderie far outweighed the general consensus of perceived injustice.

Finally I was able to appreciate some of the splendor that surrounded me. I had attained reasonable serenity, but what I needed more than ever was a plan to resume normalcy. I wanted an apartment, transportation, and the ability to recommence my employment. But I still had problems navigating the trails and rigidness of the campgrounds. Fortunately, and by God's grace, I'd managed to purchase a cellular phone. I spent the majority of my days isolated in my cabin, trying to orchestrate desired transactions via my wireless.

Occasionally, I'd make it down to the flat areas where most of the camp's amenities were located; however, my aching legs severely impeded my progress, which was why I was overjoyed when God sent another Samaritan into my life. Her name was Eloise Peters; she was white, somewhat timid but nonetheless profound. She asked if anyone needed help. I was blown away by her presence! Normally shy, I was hesitant to speak, but her demeanor compelled me. She was short in stature, much like myself, and had silver-grey hair. She was petite, wore glasses, and had a kind, maternal face. She introduced herself, and I in turn did the same. Our initial attempts at communication were awkward. But then Eloise began sharing stories about her family, grandchildren, and daily life. She was funny, sincere, and endearing. She could have been anywhere, but she was in my room, offering assistance. She and I connected immediately. Many strange things had happened to me since the onset of Katrina—amongst them miracles. And having Eloise come into my life at that precise moment certainly qualifies as a miracle! I believe that our friendship was destined.

CHAPTER 29

In mid-October 2005, the director announced that the camp would close. He advised the lingering evacuees to hasten their search for other accommodations. But we who remained were disadvantaged. Because most of us were single, FEMA had only authorized us to receive one-bedroom vouchers. And unfortunately, in the county in which we were located, one-bedroom apartments were scarcer than hen's teeth.

So we were competing with each other as well as with impossible odds. We could not return home, because news reports advised that although the waters had receded, New Orleans was still under martial law. The governor of Louisiana, the New Orleans mayor, and National Guardsmen were prohibiting citizens from returning. Moreover, the water, having stagnated for a period of over two weeks, had created serious health problems as well as extensive damage to property.

It was unhealthy for us in New Orleans and rocky for us in Arkansas; overall, our future was uncertain.. This was a momentary setback! Control was being wrestled from my grasp. It seemed not to make a difference what efforts I exhausted; the puzzle pieces would not fit. *Why is this happening?* I wondered, but then I quickly put aside martyr's thoughts as memories of the Convention Center threatened resurgence. I'd vowed then to end self-condemnation; the whipping post had to be demolished, permanently. I had to focus. I needed constructive planning.

"We can get hotel rooms," someone suggested enthusiastically. *That's right!* I thought. There had been several news reports about FEMA paying hotel rates for stranded Katrina victims. After a quick discussion amongst ourselves, we asked the camp for help in obtaining hotel rooms. Surprisingly, they agreed.

CHAPTER 30

Maybe moving into the hotel was the exact catalyst I needed. By this time, Eloise and I had become great friends. Because I was no longer under regimen of camp policy, we now had more time together and were better able to strategize. With her help, I found an available apartment and was able to purchase a reliable car. She was instrumental and inspiring. I had liked her originally because her demeanor was similar to my own. Moreover, I admired her because she was family-oriented and very active in church. Further, she was humorous, unpretentious, and sharing. I discovered her to be trustworthy and engaging; it was like having an older sister. After only a short period, it was easy to express my desires and share my innermost thoughts with her. She included me at family gatherings and invited me to worship services. Her family, friends, and fellow parishioners also welcomed me. Things were looking up; Arkansas had become my sanctuary. I'd found higher ground!

CHAPTER 31

This past fall, CNN broadcasted a special on the two-year anniversary of Hurricane Katrina. The documentary included reports of progress as well as the lack of progress in the New Orleans comeback. Of course, I did not need a news anchor to update me on these matters. I am pretty much still in the thick of things. I suppose I am one of the fortunate ones. My home in New Orleans is under contract. The rebuilding is slow but in progress. It's a well-known fact that insurance companies, contractors, and federal and local governments are major contributors to delaying the reconstruction of New Orleans. Everyone is singing, "Come back home. Louisiana wants you back!" But in reality, there is so much red tape, financial shortages, endless documents, and undesired scuttlebutt that it is extremely infuriating. I really can't see New Orleans returning to thriving community status anytime soon. Meanwhile, I am back at work, employed at Little Rock Processing and Distribution Center in Pulaski County, Arkansas.

This, too, was no easy undertaking. But by the time I reached the task of establishing reemployment, I had graciously learned to adjust and adapt. Accordingly, when the post office announced their stance to refuse my employment, I was patient. I was also a member of Eloise's church. So relying on the help of prayers, both my own and those of my fellow parishioners, I was able to "let go and let God." It took nearly eighteen months, but postal managers ultimately yielded their position. They accepted my career status and assigned me a job comparable to the duties I'd performed while in New Orleans. God is good—this was a major coup! The post office can be a dangerous opponent. I have been with them for nearly fifteen years, and I am very familiar with the term "going postal." Sometimes when there is a disagreement between managers and employees, it can drag on for years. Unfortunately, and in most cases, it is the employee who is disadvantaged during these medieval standoffs. Moreover, some conflicts have created physical and mental illness or resulted in unpredicted criminal acts. I, on the other hand, had no desire for any of these outcomes. My goal was to achieve stability. So I prayed for intervention and held on to His unchanging hand.

CHAPTER 32

I don't know how long I will be in Arkansas, but thus far, I am enjoying life. This is mainly due to my having come to terms with this unconventional yet alluring metropolis. There is still some skepticism, especially when it comes to racial issues; however, I attempt to live each day with an open mind and devoid of controversy. My attempts are not always winning, but more often than not, they are. Having survived Katrina, the Convention Center, and shelter life, I am no longer easily offended by chauvinist attitudes. After all, if it wasn't for ignorance in the first place, I would not be writing this story. Therefore, it is my belief that God has delivered me to Arkansas for a reason. Moreover, in recent months as I endeavored to capture my Katrina experience on paper, I have become more enamored of my new home. For in addition to my old friends who previously resided in New Orleans and who are now scattered throughout the United States, I have expanded my network. One can never have too many friends. Still, I miss New Orleans and plan to return one day. When folks question why I would want to go back, they ask if I am not fearful of a reoccurrence. I answer, "Yes, I am afraid, but no one can predict the future, and disasters can happen anywhere, anytime." I suppose a more truthful response would be, "There is nothing like the rapture of your own stomping grounds. The smells, the feel, the quirks and customs are all inbred characteristics of New Orleans that can never be replaced." But until then, each morning I am thankful for God's love, higher grounds, and a new beginning.

The spiritual that says, "God is an on-time god. He may not come when you call, but He's always on time" is oh so true. For during my entire journey, and every time I cried out, God answered. Even when I was in tremendous pain, severe anguish, or unable to recognized His answers, He did not forsake me. Katrina may have been devastating and destructive, but it was also a medium through which to serve God's purpose. I don't pretend to know His plans. I am just content to embrace each day with a joyous spirit and love in my heart. Moreover, I am convinced that most of my journey served to restore my vision and redefine my needs. I know that I am blessed, and I acknowledge that the world is not perfect. Each day I pray for patience and wisdom as I realize, just as Paul advised, "He is not through with me."

Printed in the United States
145632LV00005B/3/P